Demolition Woman

Annie Barksdale, Ph.D.

xulon
PRESS

Demolition Woman
by Annie Barksdale, Ph.D.

Printed in the United States of America

Library of Congress Control Number: 2002101193
ISBN 1-591600-17-0

Unless otherwise indicated, Bible quotations are taken from the King James Version.

Xulon Press
11350 Random Hills Road
Suite 800
Fairfax, VA 22030
(703) 279-6511
XulonPress.com

Dr. Annie Barksdale
P.O. Box 8028
Stamford, CT 06905
(203) 327-0681

Lori
Be Blessed.
Always.

Dr. Anne Bakulel

Preface

======================

There is a personal war between a woman and satan. A woman is more sensitive to the spiritual realm. A woman of God has antennas when it comes to sensing trouble with her children or family. A woman has always been stronger than given credit for.

All through the Bible are examples

of women that have obeyed God and caused their families and nations to escape from death and slavery. What really happened to cause people to begin to twist the role of a woman and degrade her? Women were called and used by God in the archives of the church—Old Testament and New Testament. A woman of God will continuously pray until she receives an answer from God.

There is a stigma that God has placed in a woman that cannot be broken. A woman chosen by God regardless to who believes she is called or not will prevail under the guidance of the Holy Spirit.

> *But you shall receive power, after that the Holy Ghost is come upon you; and you shall be my witnesses unto me both in Jerusalem, and in all Judea*

and in Samaria, and to the uttermost parts of the earth.

Acts 1:8

A woman that is a God-fearing woman does not give up on her family or dreams. She refuses to allow the devil to destroy her family members.

Demolition women are:

- Warriors
- Steadfast—not idle minded.
- They know the heart of God.
- Providers for their home, whether single or married.
- They will travail for their children until Christ is formed in their children.
- They will travail for their husband until Christ is

formed in him.

A woman will detect a satanic work quicker than a man. Since satan deceived Eve in the garden, the war has been on. The seed of the Woman, Jesus Christ has placed satan under your feet.

And I will put enmity between thee and the woman, and between thy seed and her seed; it shall bruise thy head, and thou shalt bruise his heel.

Gen. 3:15

A Demolition Woman walks in the authority and victory that the Lord has given her.

Victory means winning or con-quest. Overcoming an enemy or antagonist; mastery or suc-

cess in a struggle or endeavor against odds or difficulties.

It is time for you as a DEMOLI-TION WOMAN to rise up and march to the beat of victory again and take back your anointing.

Be it known satan has already been judged and sentenced, but not executed. You have power to bind up his activities. There will be a final day for him.

And the devil that deceived them was cast into the lake of fire and brimstone, where the beast and the false prophet are, and shall be tormented day and night for ever and ever.
                    Revelation 20:10

Whether in the pulpit or on your

knees, God gave you power over the enemy. You have power to take back your children from the enemy. In fact, you have power to take back your loved ones. God has given you power to snatch your family out of the hand of the enemy.

Prepare for war and conquer all. A Demolition Woman goes out with the sole purpose of winning. A Demolition Woman is not double-minded. What is she looking to win? What types of battles will she fight hardest to win? She will fight the battles against sickness, disease and war with death.

Acknowledgements

To my mother, Kara Moore, a demolition woman. She is a woman of strength, character, and a pioneer woman. She is courageous in battle and has fought the war against death many times trying to conquer her soul. She still continues to fight the good fight of faith.

To my father, Singleton Moore, who is deceased. He taught me how to survive in this world. What a mighty man of God. I learned years later more about my father's character. He was a quiet and gentle man, full of love and compassion for his family and all people.

To my sister, Barbara Ann Moore, who has in the past several years become a demolition woman (a warrior). Barbara has conquered her fears and proven to be a mighty woman of God. I have watched her grow in stature.

To my sister, Dorothy Brown, a mighty woman of God who is destined for greatness. Dorothy has encouraged me to be all that God says that I am.

To the late Kara B. Moore, my sister. What a prayer warrior. I consider her as an angel of the Lord. She was my intercessory prayer partner who I will always maintain a space in my heart for her smile, love and warmth, and the confidant she was to me. I thank God for the prophetic words that God used her to speak over my life.

To a special friend that has been there through thick and thin. A mighty woman of God with a quiet spirit, Sister Shirley Moore.

Friends are rare to find and hard to keep through years of pain and suffering. A good friend sticks closer than a brother. Thank you, Sister Margaret Campbell.

There is a special friend that would

not want me to call her name. But I must. She has been there for me. During my trials she encouraged me to look to Jesus. Sister Deloris Hill, thank you.

To my friend, Pastor Janie Watkins. We met on the mountain, we conversed in the valley and we have crossed our Jordans. Thank you for being there.

To Elder Stacey Densmore of Community Tabernacle, a great encourager who has a heart of compassion for women. Thank you for everything. To her husband, my pastor, Bishop Michael Densmore, who has a heart for God's people. Thank you.

To Elder Veronica Richards a demolition woman. Thank you for being their in crucial times. Thank you for being the encourager and prayer warrior that God has entrusted you with.

To Deaconess Cheryl Robinson, thank you for being an encourager and a mighty woman of God.

To The Women In Ministry Staff: Natalie Wiggins, Diane Patterson-Wray, Pauline Blake, Shirley Moore, Theresa Melton, Ethel Drissen, Evelyn Brown, Joan Phang, Sandra Morgan, Josie Kendall, R.J. and Lykia Kendall, Jeanette Ware, Denise Fullerton. Thank you for your support and confidence.

Table of Contents

Introduction

A DEMOLITION WOMAN is a strong warrior. A warrior is one that is engaged or experienced in warfare. A DEMOLITION WOMAN is a woman skilled in battle. She is determined, in other words, fully persuaded, in her own mind to destroy the works of the devil. She is a consistent prayer warrior sensitive to the spiritual realm. She is out to destroy the works of satan that will try to hold her or her family in captivity. A DEMOLITION WOMAN is a woman of wisdom and integrity.

She is observant. She has observed the games the enemy plays. She has watched the tactics of the enemy. She has watched the enemy prey on silly women. She has seen the cunning spirit of men that lead silly women into captivity.

> *For of this part are they who creep into houses, and lead captive silly women laden with sins away with various lusts. Ever learning, and never able to come to the knowledge of the truth.*
>
> *II Timothy 3:6-7*

A DEMOLITION WOMAN is well abreast of betrayal. She has seen double-minded women who will betray other women. The enemy placed these silly women in certain positions to buff a demolition woman who is on the frontline battlefield. The enemy usually is in the camp and seemingly a close friend.

The enemy always uses rivalry women, who are after power and recognition to undermine other women of God who are seeking to please God and bring about deliverance. It is sad when you see another woman who could be a DEMOLITION WOMAN fight against women that she knows love the Lord and are about their Father's business.

These women, because of rivalry, will try to down women leaders who God has ordained. A DEMOLITION WOMAN has more than one battle to fight and win. God has raised up demolition women for a time such as this. They are training other women to be skilled in battle, for believe it or not, there are still some wars ahead of you.

A DEMOLITION WOMAN has to be able to detect and deal with treacherous women. They walk in a familiar spirit, competing against their sisters. The sad part is, they have not prepared fully for the race. You realize, when there is a race, runners have to be prequalified. Runners do not show up at a race and say, "I want to run today." Runners have trainers and they work with them and process them to run. The trainer signs the runner up and coaches him or her for the race. Trainers will not enter a runner who is not ready or who they feel do not have as good a chance as the other runners to win.

Have we not all one father?

Hath not one God created us?
Why do we deal treacherously,
every man against his brother
by profaning the covenant of
our fathers?

Malachi 1:10

The questions asked above are still questions for today. Why can't we as the body of Christ, especially sisters, get along? It is time to stop quoting Scriptures and possess the words spoken or read. It is time for the mask to come off. It is time to walk from the slavery mentality level of distrust for each other. Bondage will remain in the mind of a woman who does not allow changes to take place and build her self-esteem. Let's not take our covenant relationship lightly.

A DEMOLITION WOMAN knows that her big brother, Jesus Christ's purpose, was to destroy the works of the devil.

> *He that committed sin is of the devil: For the devil sinneth from the beginning: For this purpose, the Son of God was manifested that he might destroy the works of the devil.*
>
> *I John 3:8*

She continues to fight because Jesus Christ endowed her with power to do greater works. A warrior fights to the finish. A warrior will not give up her post even if they are the last survivor of that battle.

A DEMOLITION WOMAN stays ready to bind up the works of the enemy. She strategically plans to weaken the forces of the enemy. She is equipped to take the territory God has promised her. Warriors warn other warriors of the enemy approaching the camp. Warriors have stood in tle in past times and will stand in th future. A DEMOLITION WOMAN knows how to fight the good fight of faith. Her ears are open to hear instructions from God. She will stand when she has no knowledge of what to do. She is courageous. She does not give up at the sight of blood.

> *Wherefore seeing we also are compassed about with so great a cloud of witnesses, let us lay aside every weight, and the sin which doth so easily beset us, and let us run with patience the race that is set before us, looking unto Jesus the author and finisher of our faith; who for the joy that was set before him endured the cross, despising the the shame, and is set down at the right hand of the*

God.

Hebrews 12:1-2

...ITION WOMAN is chosen by God. With all the perplexities and trials today, heartaches in home and in the ministry, a woman must know she is chosen by God. To remain effective, she must stay in the face of God. She must abide in the Lord and in the Word of God. When one abides, one remains in one place or state. One waits patiently for an answer. Abide also represents loyalty, faithfulness and longsuffering. This is the process that will cause a woman to become bold and strong in the Lord.

Let us, therefore, come boldly unto the throne of grace, that we may obtain mercy, and find grace to help in time of need.
Hebrews 4:16

God will not only hold your hand, He will communicate with you and help you. You must, however, trust Him. God is a Spirit, infinite, eternal and unchangeable (immutable) in His being, wisdom, power, holiness, justice, goodness and truth.

> *For there is no respect of persons with God.*
>
> *Romans 2:11*

A DEMOLITION WOMAN has been groomed to protect the innocent, weak, and destroy the plans of the enemy. She will fight for her family and your family, too. D-E-M-O-L-I-T-I-O-N W-O-M-A-N!

There are women in the Bible that were DEMOLITION WOMEN.

ATTRIBUTES OF A DEMOLITION WOMAN

- She frets not herself because of evil doers
- She is not envious of workers of iniquity
- She trusts in the Lord
- She delights herself in the Lord
- She commits her ways unto the Lord
- She rests in the Lord
- She waits patiently on the Lord
- She ceases from anger and forsakes the very appearance of wrath
- She is teachable
- She delights in the abundance of peace
- She has an wholesome conversation

- She is a satisfied woman
- She extends mercy
- She is a giver of her time, service, and money
- She allows her steps to be ordered by the Lord
- She walks in the delegated authority given her

DEBORAH
The Warrior and Judge

========================

Deborah, a prophetess and the wife of Lapidoth. She dwelt under a palm tree named Deborah between Ramah and Bethel in Mount Ephraim. Deborah was also a woman of integrity. Deborah was the leader of Israel.

Deborah was visited by the children of Israel under the tree. They would come up to her for judgement. God also gave her military strategies to inform Barak to defeat his enemies. She did not focus on the strength of the enemy, but on the instructions of God. She remained focused under opposition. Barak was under Deborah. He wanted his leader, Deborah, by his side in battle.

> *Give, therefore, thy servant an understanding heart to judge thy people, that I may discern between good and bad. For who is able to judge this thy so great a people?*
>
> *I Kings 3:9*

God raised Deborah up and gave her leadership abilities. Barak, the

2

son of Abinoam out of Kedesh-Naphtali, was a leader but fearful: He had facts about the enemy but Deborah had a relationship with God. She obeyed the instructions of God. She trusted that God's strategy was better than the enemy.

Deborah inspired Barak to fight. She gave him a prophetic word that Sisera would be delivered in his hand. She also advised him it would be done by the hand of a woman. The woman was Jael, the wife of Heber. Jael slew Sisera. Jael drove a nail through his head. She went down in history.

Barak was a man of wisdom that listen to the Deborah assigned to his life. Barak did not want to go fight the enemy without the right warrior by his side, be it male or female. In this case it was a female, Deborah. His Demolition Woman (Deborah) went with him. He followed precisely the instructions God gave her and won the battle. If you can lay aside every weight and respect the God in person—whether male or female—great battles will be won daily. Victory came back to Israel when Deborah rose up as a mother of Israel.

And Barak said unto her, If thou wilt go with me, then I will go: but If thou wilt not go with me, then I will not go.
                                        Judges 4:8

Barak met Zebulun and Naphtali at Kedesh. He went up with exactly the number he was advised to take—not one more or less than Deborah commanded him to take.

The Men of God that would allow the Deborahs of today to rise up and work along side of them will experience victories in their ministries that they could never fathom in their minds. However, the men that choose to persecute the Deborahs of today will miss a great opportunity of leadership to win the battles that are ahead of them.

Deborahs rise up and help them that desire to be helped from this day forward. Do not waste your precious time with those that do not believe in the God within you or you. Move on to those that have an ear to hear.

A warrior must keep stepping, regardless to what is going on around her. When in battle, you must keep stepping. However, don't march unprepared. Your feet have to be shod with the preparation of the Gospel.

God is the One that will drive out your enemies (Deuteronomy 7:1-6).

JAEL
Warrior

━━━━━━━━━━━━━━

Jael was a capable woman, quick, clever and fearless. Jael was considered by the Israelites as the most blessed of women. Jael, this woman of power, courage, a fulfillment of a prophetical word spoken by Deborah, was also a slayer.

Jael was the destroyer of the baddest warrior on the scene at that time, Sisera. Jael took out the most feared man and strongest man, skilled in battle and an undefeated warrior. He would be called the super power in the 21st century. The men feared him and could not conquer him. His war strategics were superb. For twenty years Sisera oppressed the children of God without mercy.

According to Judges 4:3, he had nine hundred chariots of iron. He had Israel crying out to God for a deliverer. However, this one woman skilled in battle handled the matter. Jael drove a tent nail through Sisera's head as he laid down to rest. She took him out in a heartbeat, this mighty warrior of God.

As we recapture some information. Sisera came to Jael's tent with confidence of hospitality. He even asked Jael to stand at the door of the tent and watch for him. Jael's house was considered Sisera's sanctuary at this time of refuge. Sisera did not know the one that he was asking to watch for him was the very hand that would take his life.

Before Sisera laid down to rest, Jael gave him a little milk to drink. After Sisera laid down to rest, Jael took one of the tent nails and drove it through his head.

Jael, a DEMOLITION WOMAN, is able to walk out and tell what she did to Barak. It took a lot of nerve and courage. Can you imagine this woman walking out with blood on her hand? She indeed had a powerful stature.

The angel of the Lord stated, *"Blessed above women shall Jael, the wife of Heber the Kenite be; blessed shall she be above women in the tent.*

Judges 5:24

The Kenites were a tribe to which Jethro, the father-in-law of Moses, belonged. Some dwelt amongst the Amalekites, South of Judah. The Kenites were also considered a Nomadic Tribe.

For twenty years Sisera oppressed the children of God without mercy. According to Judges 4:3, he had nine hundred chariots of iron. He had Israel crying out to God for a deliverer. But mind you, one woman—a warrior—took him down in a heartbeat.

It took only one DEMOLITION WOMAN to do what 10,000 men or more could not do.

SARAH
Noble Warrior

═══════════════

Sarah was Abraham's wife. Her name means "princess." She tried to help her husband out by giving him her handmaiden, Hagar. After Sarah gave Hagar to Abraham as a second wife, Hagar turned on Sarah. She began to make a mockery of Sarah's barrenness.

After Hagar conceived a son, Ishmael, the trouble in the household really climaxed. Ishmael and his mother became a burden in Sarah's household. This was a great test for Sarah. If you can, allow your mind to visualize a woman that you think is your servant, who will honor you and be loyal to you and then becomes your main enemy. She betrays you and makes a mockery of you. No doubt Sarah had shared many secrets with Hagar in her servitude role. You really have to be careful who you share intimacy with. They will turn on you when you least expect it.

However, Sarah takes courage and faces her issue and instructs her husband to drive this woman out of their home. No one really talks about the situation that much. But again, if you put your thinking cap on, I am sure Abraham tried more than once to get

Hagar pregnant. Somewhere in the intimacy, soul ties took place.

After all of this transpired, Sarah is told by an angel of the Lord that she will conceive a child, Sarah chuckles at the promise of God. Whether or not she believed it initially, it came to pass. Some of you have chuckled at your promise, due to the lateness of the matter.

God gave Sarah the strength to receive, conceive and deliver her promise. You see, it is not enough to receive and conceive. You must have the strength to deliver your promise and you must have the grace to raise your promise. Sarah conceived a child at the age of 90, which was the promised child "Isaac."

ABIGAIL
Brave Warrior

A bigail had good understanding. She was full of the wisdom of God. She had a beautiful countenance. However, she was married to Nabal, a man that was very evil and foolish. Nabal outright refused to supply David and his soldiers with provisions. Nabal sent David's men away empty handed.

In David's moment of anger he set out to destroy Nabal and his household. Thank God, one of the servants told Abigail how David's servants had approached Nabal correctly, however he sent them away empty-handed.

Abigail had enough sense to act without the consent of her husband when it was for his good and the good of others concerned. Abigail immediately sought to correct the matter. Abigail faced David and his army. David and his army were coming to destroy Nabal and his household.

Then Abigail made haste, and took two hundred loaves and two (skins) of wine, and five sheep ready dressed, and five measures of parched (grain), and a hundred clusters of raisins, and two hundred cakes of figs, and laid them on asses. And she said unto her servants, Go on before me: behold, I come after you. But she told not her husband, Nabal.

I Samuel 25:18-19

Abigail went to David and pleaded for mercy for her household. She also gave David some advice while she was there. A brave warrior must stay focused in the midst of problems. Abigail gave King David a word of wisdom.

The word of wisdom is a supernatural revelation by the Spirit of God concerning the divine purpose in the mind and will of God.

David was humble enough to receive it. Today if you go to some leaders to encourage them and share with them they will pretend they are listening and accepting you, and turn right back a day later at another given opportunity and let you know they're not even going to consider counsel from you. They really don't care if it's godly counsel or not. They just don't receive you. They will even try and sway the congregation not to accept you.

David, being a good leader, recognized Abigail as a woman of God. Abigail was brave and willing to die for what she believed.

And David said to Abigail, Blessed be the Lord God of Israel, who sent thee this day to meet me. And blessed be thy advice, and blessed be thou, who has kept me this day from coming to shed blood, and from avenging myself with mine own hand. For in very deed, as the Lord God of Israel liveth, who hath kept me back from hurting thee, except thou hadst hasted and come to meet me, surely there had not been left unto Nabal by the morning light any (male child). So David received of her that which had brought him, and said to her, Go up in peace to thine house; see, I have hearkened to thy voice and have accepted thy person.

I Samuel 25:32-35

When Abigail returned home, her husband was holding a great feast. He became drunk during the feast. Abigail waited until the next morning to tell him what she did in regards to David and his army. When Abigail finally told him the next morning, he became very cold within his heart. The Word states he became as stone. Ten days later the Lord killed Nabal.

And It came to pass about ten days after, that the Lord smote Nabal, that he died. And when David heard that Nabal was dead, he said, "Blessed be the Lord, who hath pleaded the cause of my reproach from the hand of Nabal, and hath kept his servant from evil; for the Lord hath returned the wickedness of Nabal upon his own head. And David sent and talked with Abigail, to take her (in marriage). And when the servants of David were come to Abigail to Carmel, they spoke unto her saying, David sent us unto thee, to take thee to him (in marriage). And she arose, and bowed herself on her face to the earth, and said, Behold, let thine handmaid be a servant to wash the feet of the servants of my lord. And Abigail hastened, and arose and rode upon an ass, with five damsels of hers who went after her; and she went after the messengers of David and became his wife.

I Samuel 25:38-42

After Nabal's death, Abigail became the wife of David. Through her bravery and good deed she ended up with a mighty man of God.

HULDAH
Prophetic Warrior

═══════════════

Huldah was the wife of Shallum the son of Tikvah, the son of Harhas, keeper of the wardrobe. Huldah destroyed the enemy's work with the knowledge of God. She was a prophetess that remained in the college in Jerusalem, a woman of knowledge.

Word of knowledge is a super-natural revelation by the Spirit of God concerning people, places or things present and past.

It's a difficult task for most men to seek counsel or wisdom from a woman. However, King Josiah sent five men to converse with Huldah, the prophetess. These men were not just ordinary men—they were men of stature. The king trusted and respected their input.

Let's take a look at who he sent. Look at their occupations. These were not ordinary men:

- Hilkiah the priest
- Ahikam the son of Shaphan
- Achbor the son of Michaiah
- Shapan the scribe
- Asahiah, a servant of the king

They communed with her as instructed. Huldah was a bold soldier of the Lord. The prophetic word she sent was not an encouraging word. It was a judgment word. It was not a word they had heard before, but it was an accurate word.

She told them to inform the king because they had worshipped idol gods. Evil was coming to them. Because of Judah's tender heart, God did not allow evil to come upon them at this time. God spared them.

LEAH
Praise Warrior

==

Leah was the oldest daughter of Laban. She was what you would consider a plain girl. Rachel was her younger sister. Rachel was considered beautiful and lovely.

Leah destroyed the very spirit of low self-esteem in her own life. Leah was a weak-eyed girl. She really was not expecting a wedding night. Jacob loved Rachel and asked her father Laban for her. Jacob worked seven years for Rachel.

Her father tricked Jacob on his wedding night and substituted Leah for Rachel. Rachel was the one that Jacob really loved. But according to the customs, the oldest daughter must wed first.

If you can imagine, Leah had a wonderful wedding night. Perhaps it was a night she had often dreamed of taking place. Her husband Jacob makes passionate love to her on her wedding night, thinking she was Rachel, the one he loved and was supposed to be his bride. Perhaps in the course of their intimacy, Jacob called Rachel's name. However, Leah did not answer him. It really must have been painful. But if you take a look at the whole picture, Leah knew she was a substitute, and she went along with Laban.

If you can consider after the wonderful night of passion, the next morning Jacob looks over and discovers his wife is not Rachel, but Leah. Can you see him looking at her with disgust in his eyes—perhaps even throwing up along side the bed out of anguish. He realized he had made love on his wedding night to the wrong woman.

Rachel is in the other tent, angry, frustrated, bitter and upset. She now is at rivalry with her sister, Leah. Rachel hates Leah—not that they got along that great before this episode transpired. Leah is now in an awkward position. She has experienced her wedding night and now feels ashamed of hurting her sister. On the other hand, she still had a wonderful wedding night.

Jacob immediately goes to his father-in-law Laban and requests for Rachel's hand in marriage. He has to work seven more years for Rachel.

When God saw how much Leah was hated, He opened her womb. Leah was looked upon by God as barren and hated. God decides to open her womb. Yes, God decided to do something about Leah's situation.

God opened Leah's womb and kept Rachel barren for a season. Leah has her first son Reuben, which means, "Behold, a son." Leah feels now her husband will love her.

Leah now has a second son Simeon, meaning "God has heard." Leah feels the Lord heard her cry. She felt the Lord knew she was hated.

Leah now bears a third son Levi, meaning "joined." She felt Jacob would now be bonded or joined to her.

Leah is now on her fourth pregnancy and she's now in the place to seek the face of the Lord. Leah is now dealing with her self-image. She is now seeking the Lord's face.

She is a woman that is scorned by her husband—the only man she had ever been with—and her sister Rachel is now sharing her man. Leah did not ask for these problems. Leah was thrown into a marriage and all these situations by her father Laban.

Her fourth son is called Judah, meaning "God would lead." Leah's state of mind is, "Now I will praise the Lord." Her confession is also, "Now my husband will love me. I've given him a fourth son. But, just in case he does not love me, it is well with my soul." Leah's new attitude is to glorify her heavenly father.

Leah is now pregnant again with a fifth son, Issachor, meaning "strong and a server of others." Although there are issues, Jacob keeps coming back to the bed with Leah.

Leah has a sixth son, Zebulum, meaning "seafarer."

Leah has a daughter, Dinah. Dinah was raped and avenged by her brothers Simeon and Levi.

Leah's maid bore Jacob two sons also: Gad, which means "would be an overcomer in the end," and Asher, meaning "successful tiller of soil."

In Rachel's hatred of Leah, she gave her maid Bilhah to Jacob. Bilhah's sons' names were Dan, meaning "judge his people," and Naphtali, meaning "a venturesome spirit."

God remembered Rachel and she had two sons. Rachel stole her father's gods. Laban accused Joseph of stealing his gods. Rachel is the one that stole her father's gods.

Rachel's first son was Joseph, meaning "fruitful bough, blessed by the Almighty." Rachel's second son was Benjamin (Benoni), "son of my sorrow." Rachel died at childbirth. Jacob changed Benoni's name to Benjamin, meaning "son of my right hand—blessed." He was aggressive as a wolf.

In enduring all of this, Leah still went down as a matriarch. Leah was blessed after all. She learned to praise the Lord through it all. She became a Demolition Woman. She destroyed the fears in her life and low self-esteem.

This was done by seeking the face of God and acknowledging that He is a rewarder of them that diligently seek Him.

HANNAH
Prayer Warrior

===============

Hannah's name means "grace and favor." Hannah was a griever. She was fruitless (natural) barren. She grieved because she was childless. Hannah was provoked to obtain her destiny. Hannah had a glimpse and prophesied about the Messiah.

Hannah's husband, Elkanah, loved

her. However, he was unable to comfort her. Elkanah means "God has possessed." He was the father of Samuel. He was a good husband. He gave Hannah a double portion. However, Hannah was still taunted by his other wife, Peninnah. Hannah shed many tears.

Hannah was a prayer warrior. Her priest did not even know who she was. Her own priest marked her. He judged her to be in error. He judged her to be drunk. He was yet drunken with the cares of his own life. His sons were not in a spiritual place to know the difference between the spirit and flesh. He misjudged Hannah. Here is where the integrity comes in. Hannah was not arrogant. Hannah however, handled it gracefully and redeemed favor.

- *Hannah does not disrespect*

her priest, although he was out of order falsely accusing her.

- *Hannah makes a vow to God.*
- *Her vow is if He gives her a son she would give him to the Lord all the days of his life.*

She gently states, "I've emptied my soul before the Lord." Hannah's warfare was in the Spirit. Each year when she went up to the Lord's house, she was provoked and persecuted by her rival, Peninnah. Peninnah year by year strived to excel Hannah. When there is a rival, you have two people competing to reach something that only one can possess.

RIVALS

HANNAH	PENINNAH
Barren	Fruitful
Loved	Accepted
Grace	Bitter woman
Emptied	Full of Stuff
Spiritual	Natural
Worthy Portion	Portion
Griever	Hannah's Adversary

Hannah wept and did not eat, emptying her soul before the Lord. Hannah had become bitter. She prayed until she got it out of her soul. There are eight types of tears of Hannah:

1 Faith   Mark 9:24
2 Humility   Luke 7:38
3 Service   Acts 2:19
4 Admonition   Acts 20:31

5 Concern   II Corinthians 2:4
6 Sympathy   II Timothy 1:4
7 Earnest
  Supplication   Hebrews 5:7
8 Tears of
  Disappointment   Hebrews 12:17

Hannah's womb was closed by God. She was not barren.It was at Shiloh that Hannah received the promise of a son. God opens her womb because she provoked Him to release her. Eli the prophet encouraged Hannah to believe that the Lord would grant her prayer. The God of Israel granted her petition which she asked of Him. Hannah confessed that the Lord had granted her petition.

In due season Hannah had Samuel, whose name means "the Lord heard."

When she had weaned Samuel, she left him at Shiloh with the Prophet Eli. Samuel was placed in Eli's house for further training. Samuel was not born out of Eli's house, but he was anointed. She also took with her:

- Three bullocks represented offering for sin
- Flour representing manna (Bread of Life)
- Bottle of wine representing new life

Hannah received a fivefold blessing. Five more children were born: three sons and two daughters.

RAHAB
Survivor Warrior

═══════════════════

Rahab's profession is not one to be desired. However, her vocation became helpful. Her vocation enabled her to hide two of Joshua's spies in Jericho. She was willing to lose her life to protect men of God. She hid them under piles of flax on her roof when soldiers come to look for them.

Mind you, she told the soldiers that the spies had already left. Rahab had to recognize that these men were coming back to take the city. She made her request known. She asked for safety from the Israelite army in exchange for saving the spies, and they assured her she would be safe if she hung a red rope (symbolic of the blood and passing over) in her window for identification.

Rahab had to be a strong woman because she helped the spies escape by letting them down by a rope through a window in the city wall.

Warriors must possess the skill to transmit to others the message. Good communication is a serious area that most people have problems with. Rahab transmitted to the spies her desire.

Rahab and her family were the only

residents of Jericho who were permitted to live after the Battle of Jericho. Rahab later married a man of the tribe of Judah, for she is included in the genealogy in the first chapter of Matthew. Yes, Rahab the former prostitute, was the mother of Boaz, an ancestor of David and of our Savior Jesus Christ.

MARY
THE MOTHER
OF JESUS
Courageous
Warrior

———————————

Mary grew as any young girl of that time grew. She was hand picked by God to conceive His son.

Her family background traced all the way back to Abraham.

Mary, a young girl not married was told she was going to have a holy child. It has been stated by scholars that Mary was perhaps about fourteen years of age at that time. Mary was a faithful young woman. The archangel Gabriel delivered the message to Mary.

And the angel came in unto her and said, Hail, thou that art highly favoured, the Lord is with thee: blessed art thou among women.

And when she saw him, she was troubled at his saying, and cast in her mind what manner of salutation this should be.

And the angel said unto her, Fear not, Mary: for thou hast found favour with God.

*And, behold, thou shalt con-
ceive in thy womb, and bring
forth a son, and shalt call his
name JESUS.*

St. Luke 1:28-31

To be willing to accept this mission
knowing that if anyone finds out you
could be killed. Mary questions the
angel knowing she had not been with
a man.

*Then said Mary unto the
angel, How shall this be, seeing I know not a man?*

*And the angle answered and
said unto her, The Holy Ghost
shall come upon thee, and the
power of the Highest shall
overshadow thee: therefore
also that holy thing which
shall be born of thee shall be*

called the Son of God.
St. Luke 1:34-35

However, Mary considers it an honor to have the favor of God. She could have decided no or to take her life. But she rejoiced at the fact she was chosen. The angel gave specific instructions. There was clarity in this matter. Let's take another look at this. God sent an angel directly to Mary to reveal to her His plan of the Savior.

He did not tell her father or husband to be. God directly sent his messenger to Mary. Mary the mother of Jesus was a very unique woman chosen by God, to love and nurture His son. Mary pondered in her heart the things spoken by the Holy Spirit to her. She accepted the word and conceived the holy child, Jesus Christ. God called Mary as a warrior to:

- Receive the Word
- Conceive the Word
- Carry the Word
- Deliver the Word
- Watch the Word
- Submit to the Word
- Acknowledge the Word

Mary is also informed that her cousin Elizabeth, who was barren, was also six months pregnant. You know Mary had to go and check this out for her self. When she arrived, the baby in Elizabeth's womb, John the Baptist, acknowledged the Savior, Jesus Christ, that was on the inside of Mary's womb. They had a praise service inside.

Cousin Elizabeth confirms to Mary that the child she is carrying is a holy child, Jesus. John the Baptist leaped in his mother womb for joy. I often state the babies had the anointing before there mothers. The seed was given by God and breathed on by the Holy Spirit.

> *But when the fulness of the time was come, God sent forth his Son, made of a woman, made under the law,*
> *To redeem them that were under the law, that we might receive the adoption of sons.*
> *Galatians 4:4-5*

At the wedding in Cana, Mary pushed Jesus forth to work a miracle before time. He said it was not His hour. He however, could not refuse His mother. Mary understood Jesus' purpose. She journeys from birth, grave and resurrection with her Son.

In Jesus' seven last words, He gives

his mother a salutation. To Mary: Woman, behold thy son! To John: Behold thy mother!

When Jesus therefore saw his mother, and the disciple standing by, whom he loved, he saith unto his mother, Woman, behold thy son!

Then said he to the disciple, Behold thy mother! And from that hour that disciple took her unto his own home.

John 19: 26-27

While talking with a man recently about Mary, the mother of Jesus, he was not aware Jesus had other brothers and sisters. The question came to mind how many people are unaware of Jesus' siblings. Most people only see Mary as the Virgin Mary. As you read in the Word of God, your aware-

ness will come open to Mary's child-
hood, motherhood and sisterhood.

MARY MAGDALENE Warrior

================

A former prostitute before meeting Jesus. Delivered from seven demons. She became a follower of Jesus Christ. She was present at His crucifixion.

And many women were there beholding afar off, which followed Jesus from Galilee, ministering unto him:

Among which was Mary Magdalene, and Mary the mother of James and Joses, and the mother of Zebedee's children.

Matthew 27:55-56

Mary Magdalene was one of the women who first found out that Jesus had been raised from the dead.

Jesus taught the women and explained to them in Galilee that He would be delivered up and crucified, but on the third day He was raised again. The angels reminded the women of this at that grave site. Mary Magdalene ran to inform the eleven that Jesus was not in the tomb.

It was Mary Magdalene and Joanna,

and Mary the mother of James, and other women that were with them, which told these things unto the apostles.

The angel of the Lord, which are messengers, informed Mary Magdalene and the women the instructions of the Lord. Let's look at the instructions:

- Fear not
- Go quickly (don't hesitate)
- Tell His disciples (the men) He is risen from the dead
- They departed with (fear) reverence and great joy
- They ran to bring the good news

God could count on them to do the job. Women rarely forget instructions.

Jesus appeared to Mary Magdalene and commissioned her to go to the disciples and tell them he would meet them in Galilee. He also met the other women and gave them the same message to take to the disciples. Isn't it amazing? He sends one woman to tell His disciples and then He sends the second group of women to tell the disciples the same thing.

Remember, there was a company of women that He traveled with and taught. Could this be that Jesus was introducing **Women In Ministry** *to the men back at the tomb? He gave them the first ministry to take the good news of His resurrection affirmation to the disciples.*

ESTHER
Skilled Warrior

———————————

Esther's (Hadassah) name means a star, a Jewish maiden.

Esther replaced Queen Vashti, King Ahasuerus' former wife. Esther was a prayer warrior and spokeswoman for her nation.

Esther was trained by Mordecai, her uncle. Esther's parents were dead.

Esther had an advantage over most handmaids Her uncle taught her how to walk in stature as a godly woman. She was trained by a holy man. Mordecai took her as his daughter. God placed Esther in the king's house for such a time that the Jewish community would not be depleted. She was used to stop her people from being massacred by Haman. With wisdom, the one that had intended to set a trap for Mordecai got snagged in his own trap. Lesson learned: Do not dig holes for other people. You will fall in the hole yourself that you dug for someone else.

God used Esther to call a fast and she decided she would go before the king. She had an attitude of victory: "If I perish, I perish, but I am going to see the king." She adorned herself properly and entered in gracefully so that the king had to give her an audience. Haman and his ten sons were hanged as a result of her plea to the king. Most fail to realize that in this war you must be skilled; you must know how to approach the King of Kings.

It is not so much the weaponry as the skills in using the weaponry. The approach to the king is very important.Your deliverance weighs in the approach to the King of Kings. Some of us have missed and misplaced our blessings by the approach we made.

Thank God we learn from our mistakes and He is the God of a second, third and more chance(s). Esther shows forth great courage in the fact that she is ready to lose her life to save her people. If we only had a half dozen valiant women today that would give their life for righteousness. We would see a great turn of the century.

TAMAR
Righteous Warrior

Tamar marries Judah's son Er, who was wicked in the sight of God. God slew him. Tamar is left a widow and given to marry Er's brother Onan.

Onan didn't mind going in and having sex with Tamar. He refused to give seed to his brother. He felt he was not getting anything out of it for himself except pleasure.

He avoided his martial respon-
sibility. It displeased God and He
destroyed his seed. The spilling of the
seed was an abomination unto God. It
was considered breaking the law of
reproduction. It mainly displeased
God because it was stopping a con-
tinuation of Himself in mankind. He
killed Onan for touching the beginning (the seed). With every seed God
starts all over again.

A seed is a source of beginning. To
plant (sow), to remove the seed from
(the fruit (the propagating system).

Judah was a kingly seed, fourth son
of Leah and Jacob. Judah was born
out of turmoil, rejection, confusion,
dismay, resentment and loneliness. A
relationship with God will bring all of
that out. Judah advises Tamar to:

- Remain a widow. He gave

her false hope.
- Remain at her father's house, which was the place of betrayal.
- Remain until Shelah, the younger son, was grown. This was false hope.
- Tamar dwelled at her father's house.

Judah's wife, Shua's daughter died. Judah is comforted. Shelah is grown and Tamar is not his bride. Someone tells Tamar Judah is going up to shear sheep. Tamar's mindset is that Judah broke a promise. It is now pay-up time.

Tamar understands the levitical law pertaining to marriage and the next of kin. She decides to pose as a harlot.

Judah's lust took over him and he took her for a harlot. She asked for a fee. Nothing is free. If you get something free there is still upkeep fees. The price was a kid (a young goat). We know a goat is symbolic of sin, sinner's offering. Tamara understands the Law. Judah asked what pledge he should give.

She received the following:

- Thy signet – Which represented ring (covenant, position).
- Thy bracelets – Which represented position and friendship.
- Thy staff – Thy authority, power, rulership, kingship, strength, guidance.

Judah was not able to transact any business while this remained unsettled. Because of his flesh he gave his position, friendship and authority up for a one-night stand.

Tamar put away her harlot uniform. Judah didn't even go to pay his bill. He sent his friend Hirah to handle it. However, he could not find her.

Hirah asked the men where the harlot was. The men let him know there was no harlot at this place. Who would know if there was a harlot in the neighbor hood? The men. They are the ones that generally use her services. Since the men stated there was no harlot in this place, it was evident that something out of the ordinary had taken place.

Judah did not want his business in the street. Therefore, he sent his trusted friend, Hirah. Judah had a flesh weakness. He needed the companion of a woman. This is very strange how Judah let his flesh dictate to him out of need for intimacy so that he did not recognize the woman he was making love to.

You see, fleshly desires will cause one to take off their priestly garment of praise and their priestly robe of righteousness. Tamar placed her widow's garment back on. Three months later the word was in the street that Tamar was pregnant.

Like David, Judah, because of his bitterness and undealt with issues, pronounces judgement himself. You see, word got back to Judah that Tamar his daughter-in-law had played the role of a harlot. Tamar was not a harlot; she had played the harlot. We have all types of players in the house of God. The news carried as unusual. Bad news travels fast. The news is that Tamar played a harlot and she is with child out of whoredom.

Judah, in his angry state, commented, "Bring her to me. Let her be burned." He was still angry because of his sons' deaths. He blamed Tamar when it was God that killed them for their wickedness.

Let's for a moment consider Judah and how outraged he is. Yes, Judah the praiser. He is walking around for months. He can't close any deals because he has no signet (ring). He is out of fellowship (no bracelets). He is out of power (no staff). All of the items represent his leadership and authority. Judah wanted Tamar killed. Judah had a secret thought against Tamar. He thought she was the cause of his two sons' deaths and he refused to have a third son die. Therefore, he reneged on his promise.

When you hold back your seed, you will pay a great price. Tamar's intention was to force Judah to perform the levitical duty. In pre-mosiac times, every member of the late husband's family was under that obligation.

Tamar was not an ignorant woman.

She was fully abreast of what she was doing and her purpose for it.

She was promised a husband and she came to collect by whatever means necessary to bring forth her promise.

When the time of confrontation comes, again, Tamar is yet a lady. She doesn't holler or scream. She brought the evidence with her of who the father of her babies was. Tamar stated that the man that these pledges belonged to was her babies' father.

Judah acknowledges the evidence. He also acknowledges that Tamar was more righteous than he was. It is amazing how much a man will give up for a one-night stand. He'll give up his inheritance and family just for one night of sex with a woman. In spite of Judah's sexual carelessness, he showed real nobility when confronted by Tamar. Although Tamar laid with him that night, he indicated she was more righteous than he was.

The lineage of Christ came from one of the babies. The birth of the babies is a miracle. We all know how important a midwife is at the time of birth. The midwife that birthed these babies became baffled. She ties a scarlet thread symbolic of a covenant and sin offering and first born around the first hand that stuck out. However, the baby stuck his hand back in the womb and the last baby came out first.

You see, it's not who you think is righteous or first., but who God chooses to be first. He'll back up everything until His chosen one comes forth. It was God's plan. The last became first, Pharez (Mary the mother of Jesus came as a descendant) Luke 3:33. The last to actually be born was Zerah, which should have been first, but he reached back and Pharez passed him.

Jesus came from this heritage. It took great courage on Tamar's part to face the man that loved you passionately for a one-night stand and he does not recognize you when he sees you again, but would like you burned. This warrior fought the good fight of faith, not only for herself but her unborn babies at that time. She was fighting for three lives. Again, she was not a silly woman. She took the necessary tools. She must have preceived trouble was going to come out of this. I think she really knew her father-in-law had issues against her. The possessions she collected were her refuge.

NAOMI
Faith Warrior

D uring a period of famine, Naomi, Her husband Elimelech and their two sons Mahlon and Chilion, left their home town of Bethlehem and moved eastward beyond the Dead Sea to the mountain plateau of Moab. There Elimelech, Naomi's husband, died. You can see it left her grievous and lonely. The sons married Moabite girls, Orpah and Ruth. Ten years later both sons died. Now there are three despaired women.

Imagining the state of Naomi's mind at this time. She decides to leave the area, which has too many memories of grief. Naomi heard that the Lord had visited His people. She tells her daughters-in-law to remain with their families. It was quite an emotional time with tears. Naomi told her daughters-in-law she could not produce any more sons to replace their dead husbands, in so many words there was no need for them to come with her. She had nothing natural to offer them.

Orpah returned to her family, but Ruth was persistent. Ruth wanted to be with her mother-in-law, Naomi. Naomi tells her how her sister-in-law

Orpah has gone back to her people and their gods. Naomi informed Ruth she could do the same. In Ruth 1:16-19, Ruth makes some powerful statements that stirs the heart of Naomi. In other words, the relationship was great, but it was going to become greater. Look at what Ruth communicates to her mother-in-law:

- Entreat me not to leave thee or turn away from following thee.
- Where thou goest, I will go.
- Where thou lodgest, I will lodge.
- Thy people shall be my people.
- Thy God shall be my God.

Naomi discerned Ruth was steadfastly determined to go with her. She then ceased from trying to discourage her to leave. Naomi had the type of faith that will cause you to go on with your life in spite of perplexities, distresses and the death of a loved one or other problems. Naomi is a light bearer and example Ruth chooses to follow.

Therefore, my beloved brethren, be ye stedfast, unmoveable, always abounding in the work of the Lord, forasmuch as ye know that your labour is not in vain in the Lord.
I Corinthians 15:58

The relationship was so special between Ruth and Naomi. Ruth became head of household, working until evening gleaning in the field to support her mother-in-law. After working in the field, she returned home and beat the corn into barley. Good news traveled how Ruth cared for her mother-in-law, Naomi. Because of her diligence and faithfulness, Boaz, who was a kinsman to Naomi, told her not to glean another field, but remain in his field. He also instructed his servants to drop extra corn for her to glean.

It was a custom ordained by Moses. Anything left in the field was free for the poor to harvest and keep. The farmer was discouraged from reaping his entire crop because it would deprive the needy of food, according to Deuteronomy 24:19-21, which speaks of leaving a portion for the fatherless, strangers and widows.

When thou cuttest down thine harvest in thy field, and hast forgot a sheaf in the field, thou shalt not go again to fetch: it shall be for the stranger. For the fatherless, and for the

widow: that the Lord thy God may bless thee in all the work of thine hands.
Deuteronomy 24:19

Naomi not only instructed Ruth spiritually, but she naturally taught her courtship principles. She commanded her in Ruth 3:3: *Wash thyself, therefore, anoint thyself, and put thy raiment upon thee, and get thee down to the floor; but make not thyself known to the man, until he shall have finished eating and drinking.*

Naomi instructed Ruth of the custom to uncover his feet and lie down at his feet and he will instruct you what to do. Ruth had such a relationship with her mother-in-law. She told Naomi, "I will do all you command me." Ruth followed her instructions. Boaz received Ruth and told her he knew she was a virtuous woman;

however, there was a closer kinsman than him.

He would not allow her to return home empty-handed. The amazing part is the communication Ruth and Naomi had. Ruth told Naomi everything. Naomi consoled her and told her Boaz would not rest until the matter was resolved that day. Boaz followed the custom and drew off his shoes. He became the next in line for the kinsman redemption. Boaz married Ruth. Ruth bore a son. Naomi had an heir and became the child's nurse. It was because of Naomi's enduring faith. She remained faithful under suffering and misfortunes.

But the God of all grace, who hath called us into his eternal glory by Christ Jesus, after that ye have suffered a while, make you perfect, stablish, strengthen, settle you.

I Peter 5:10

LYDIA
Warrior

═══════════════════════════

Lydia was a businesswoman; a
seller of purple in the city of
Thyatira. Paul was teaching the
women by a riverside in Philippi.
While Paul was teaching the women,
Lydia, a worshipper of God, heard the
Word. Lydia led the women that met
for prayer.

At Philippi, the first partakers of the Gospel were women. Lydia started the first church in Europe.

Lydia is stated to be Paul's first convert. She was the first to be baptized, the first to open her house for church services. It was the first church formed amongst women in her house that prayed for Paul and Silas when they were in prison. Lydia is the pastor of the Philippian church.

Paul was satisfied with the Christian life exemplified in the church at Philippi. This church gave Paul the greatest comfort in his apostleship.

Lydia had two deaconesses that had issues: Euodia and Syntyche. Apostle Paul sends a letter addressing the contention between the two and encouraging them to reconcile and continue the work of the ministry.

Lydia continued influencing the church and congregations giving towards Paul. Lydia cared for Paul's welfare.

PHOEBE
New Testament
Warrior

═══════════════════

Phoebe is a Christian woman who had a ministry at the church in Cenchrea. She was chosen to assist in the church ministry. She assisted in the daily administration and helped ministry. Phoebe understood her position and walked worthy.

Paul had Phoebe deliver the epistle to the Romans. You should understand, Paul sent a woman to take the word to the church.

> *I commend unto you Phoebe our sister, which is a servant of the church which is at Cenchrea: That ye receive her in the Lord, as becometh saints, and that ye assist her in whatsoever business she hath need of you: for she hath been a succorer of many, and of myself also.*
>
> *Romans 16:1-2*

Phoebe protected Paul and many. Anyone serving as a protector for another must be equipped as a warrior.

DORCAS (TABITHA)
Warrior

═══════════════════

Dorcas was a Christian woman in Joppa. Dorcas is referred to as a disciple. She was a leader in the Christian community. She was a woman full of good works. She was also a seamstress that clothed people.

It is apparent that Dorcas had favor in the community. She was always there helping in whatever manner necessary to improve her community.

They had washed Dorcas' body and prepared for the mourners to come in.

The widows had already positioned themselves. However, Peter came in and upset their funeral arrangements. In fact, Peter put them out, prayed and commanded Tabitha to arise.

But Peter put them all forth, and kneeled down, and prayed; and turning him to the body said, Tabitha, arise. And she opened her eyes: and when she saw Peter, she sat up. And he gave her his hand, and lifted her up, and when he had called the saints and widows, presented her alive.

Acts 9:40-41

Dorcas was returned by Peter to her community to continue the good works she was providing for her community.

PRISCILLA
Warrior

Priscilla was a Christian woman who with her husband Aquila labored alongside Paul at Corinth.

And Paul after this tarried there yet a good while, and then took his leave of the brethren, and sailed thence into Syria, and with him Priscilla and Aquila; having shorn his head in Cenchrea: for he had a vow. And he came to Ephesus, and left them there: but he himself entered into the synagogue, and reasoned with the Jews.

Acts 18:18-19

Priscilla is named before her husband in the majority of passages, which indicates her strength and position of character in Christian work. Priscilla and her husband were also tent makers.

They had a church in their house at Ephesus. Paul commends them in Romans and expresses his gratitude for Priscilla and Aquila.

Greet Priscilla and Aquila my helpers in Christ Jesus: Who have for my life laid down their own necks: unto whom not only I give thanks, but also all the churches of the Gentiles. Likewise greet the church that is in their house. Salute my well-beloved Epaenetus, who is the first fruits of Achaia unto Christ.

Romans 16:3-5

Priscilla and Aquila were very instrumental in the training of Apollos. Apollos needed further discipleship and knowledge of the word of God.

The Calling Forth of Prayer Warriors

―――――――――

The Old Testament speaks of the cunning women (praying women) to come forth and intercede in prayer. Prayer is the process of seeking the will of God in one's life. Prayer is communicating with God.

But ye, beloved, building up

yourselves on your most holy faith, praying in the Holy Ghost.

Jude 20

The prayer warrior's main objective is to lift up the name of Jesus. When one lifts up, one raises from a lower position to a higher position. Lifting also denotes moving from one position to another position.

And I, If I be lifted up from the earth, will draw all men unto me.

John 12:32

We have to shout the name of Jesus in our families, place to place, in the atmosphere and above the enemy.

When we lift up the name of Jesus, we prepare an entrance for our blessing. Although we may not need the same type of blessing today, we need a blessing. You have overcome satan. You see, you may not need finances. You need a healing. Then again, you may not need healing. You need money. You could conceivably need an attitude adjustment.

The need is as never before today for women to come together and strengthen one another in prayer and supplication for our families and nation. We need in this hour plain, simple communication, sharing our fears and disappointments with one another and praying that our Father will give us the faith and integrity to move forth.

Our nation is faced with issues they knew would eventually hit our shores. Now our nation has to readjust its mode of living, thinking, security and weaponry.

Many homes are faced with problems still such as teenage pregnancy, drugs, AIDS, children running away from home, husbands failing to assume their responsibilities and the burden of single parent homes.

Your hearts bleed, you feel you are the only one facing these types of issues. Beloved, there are many that are faced with these same issues or going through similar situations, if not more intense.

Many married couples are contemplating divorce. Everyone wants out today of unfilled relationships. There are just as many Christians divorcing and remarrying as the secular today. Could it be the Church has become too worldly and has picked up the same lustful desires of the world? Could it be the church now longs for fulfillment of the flesh more than holiness?

If you can find the strength to

focus on Jesus Christ and become an active member in the ministry of Jesus Christ, fulfillment will come. It's going to take commitment in your home and in the ministry of Jesus Christ—a ministry where Jesus Christ is the Chief Shepherd and the pastor is the under-shepherd and has a love for souls.

This is not the time to quit. This is the glorious time to brace yourself, focus, zero in on your prize and walk towards it with victory in Christ Jesus. This is discovery time. Seek the face of God for your purpose and go for it.

A Warrior's Keys

And I will give unto thee the keys of the kingdom of heaven: and whatsoever thou shalt bind on earth shall be bound in heaven: and whatsoever thou shall loose on earth shall be loosed in heaven.

Matthew 16:19

Keys represent the authority to enter and exit. The person that has the keys is going to open the doors entrusted. Keys were generally worn over one's shoulder. We know the shoulders represent government. It's time to use the keys the Master has given you. The Master has given you the power to bind and loose.

And the key of the house of David will I lay upon his shoulder: so he shall open, and none shall shut: and he shall shut, and none shall open.

Isaiah 22:22

In other words, God is letting you

know heaven agrees with what you bind and loose according to the Word and will of God. If you bind and loose on earth, it is bound and loosed in heaven. When one binds, it means to constrain with legal authority; to hinder from operation and to restrict the opponent's movement. To loose means to permit freedom; to free from restraint; to release; to set free from a state of confinement or restraint.

> *Verily I say unto you, Whatsoever ye shall bind on earth shall be bound in heaven: and whatsoever ye shall loose on earth shall be loosed in heaven.*
> *Matthew 18:18*

As a warrior in this generation, you have keys to enter into your destiny. It is going to take focusing on the instructions that God has given you and using your keys to enter in. The Word of God has informed us; however, we must believe.

> *And all things whatsoever ye shall ask in prayer, believing, ye shall receive.*
> *Matthew 21:22*

> *Jesus said unto him, If thou canst believe, all things are possible to him that believeth.*
> *Mark 9:23*

Prayer is essential in your Christian walk and life. Jesus has insured you He will do it for you. With the keys you also have wisdom, understanding, counsel, might, knowledge, the fear of the Lord, judgement and reproof.

And the spirit of the Lord *shall rest upon him, the spirit of wisdom and understanding, the spirit of counsel and might, the spirit of knowledge and of the fear of the* Lord; *And shall make him of quick understanding in the fear of the* Lord: *and he shall not judge after the sight of his eyes, neither reprove after the hearing of His ear. But with righteousness shall he judge the poor, and reprove with equity for the meek of the earth:and he shall smite the earth: with the rod of his mouth, and with the breath of his lips shall he slay the wicked.*

Isaiah 11:2-4

If ye shall ask anything in my

name, I will do it.

John 14:14

Did you know that you can have the keys but not the power to open your door? If you are going to be a DEMOLITION WOMAN (warrior) for Christ you must be filled with the Holy Spirit. In fact, without the Holy Spirit you do not have the power or ability to use your keys.

But ye shall receive power, after that the Holy Ghost is come unto you: and ye shall be witnesses unto me both in Jerusalem, and in all Judah and in Samaria and unto the uttermost part of the earth.

Acts 1:8

As a warrior with boldness and faith, you have a right to use the keys.

You need power to guard your Spirit. It is very important that you hear truth—the Word of God. Your spirit must hear the Word. The Word must be presented by an anointed oracle of God.

A Warrior's Strength

A good warrior realizes that strength comes from God. In order for a Christian to be strong in the Lord, they must put on the whole armor of God for spiritual battle. A warrior must be stedfast.

Stand fast therefore in the lib-

erty wherewith Christ hath made us free, and be not entangled again with the yoke of bondage.

Gal. 5:1

A warrior is not bound or constrained. Paul addresses the Christians to hold fast to their personal liberty, which is God's grace. He was allowing them to know they were not saved by the keeping of the mosaic law, but by the precious blood of Jesus. For without the shedding of blood there is no remission. Jesus Christ was the fulfillment of the law. Now He is our High Priest. As a warrior you must stand fast:

- In Faith – *But without faith it is impossible to please him; for he that cometh to God must believe that he is a rewarder of them that diligently seek him. Hebrews 11:6*

- In Liberty – Your authority as a believer free from the law. *For brethren ye have been called unto liberty; only use not liberty for an occasion to the flesh, but by love, serve one another. Gal. 5:13*

- In the Spirit – *If we live in the Spirit, let us walk in the Spirit. Gal. 5:25*

A Warrior is free in Christ, yet accountable to God. A great price has been paid in full. Therefore, let us walk in the freedom and not live loose, but free to walk in the Spirit, and we will not fulfill the lust of the flesh. A Warrior must be focused at all times. A Warrior is able to soar above the trials, having the peace on God in the midst of a storm.

A Warrior's Armor

---

*Finally my brethren be strong
in the Lord and in the power
of his might.*

Ephesians 6:10

A Demolition Woman is a woman
of weaponry that knows how to

use her weapons. She wears her armor well and she keeps her armor on. She places her helmet on to protect her mind and renew her mind. She wears the breastplate of righteousness to guard her heart. Her shield is the Shield of Faith used to protect her body. The shield of faith protects and defends her from the arrows seen and unseen.

She girds her loins about with truth. She protects her legs. She walks with her sword on her side. She never leaves home without the Word. She walks in the Word of God. She meditates in the Word of God day and night. Her feet are shod with the preparation of the Gospel. She walks in the anointing of God and the Peace of God. She uses the sword of the Spirit, which is the Word of God, when the enemy attacks.

For the word of God is quick, and powerful, and sharper than any twoedged sword, piercing even to the dividing asunder of soul and spirit, and of the joints and marrow, and is a discerner of the thoughts and intents of the heart.

Hebrews 4:12

A DEMOLITION WOMAN IS STRONG IN THE LORD.

When a strong man, fully armed, guards his house, even his possessions are safe.

Luke 4:21

DEMOLITION WOMAN IS FULLY COMMITTED AND POSSESSES THE FOLLOWING QUALITIES:

- FAITH – *But without faith it*

is impossible to please him. For he that cometh to God must believe that he is, and that he is a rewarder of them that diligently seek him. Hebrews 11:6

- UNDERSTANDING – *He that hath knowledge spared his words; and a man of understanding is one of an excellent spirit. Proverbs 17:27*

- UNMOVEABLE – *Therefore, my beloved brethren, be ye stedfast, unmoveable, always abounding in the work of the Lord, for as much as ye know that your labor is not in vain in the Lord. I Corinthians 15:58*

- LOVING – *He that loveth not knoweth not God, for God is love. I John 4:8*

- LISTENER – *For I will speak excellent things and the opening of my lips shall be right things. Proverbs 8:34*
- YIELDED – *And sow the fields, and plant vineyards, which may yield fruits of increase. Psalm 107:37*
- CONVERSATIONIST – *Seeing then that all these things shall be dissolved. What manner of persons ought ye to be in all holy, conversation and godliness. II Peter 3:11*
- OBEDIENT – *Obedience is better than sacrifice. I Samuel 15:22.*
- MERCIFUL – *Be ye therefore merciful, as your Father also is merciful. Luke 6:36*

- MODERATE – *Let your moderation be known unto all men. The Lord is at hand. Philippians 4:5*
- INTERCESSOR – *I exhort therefore that first of all, supplications, prayers, intercessions, and giving of thanks, be made for all men. II Timothy 2:1*
- TEMPERANCE (SELF-CONTROL) – *Meekness, temperance:against such there is no law. Galatians 5:23*
- TACTFUL – *It is a sport to a fool to do mischief. But a man of understanding hath wisdom. Proverbs 10:23*
- ENCOURAGER – *…but David encouraged himself in the Lord his God. I Samuel 30:6*

- DILIGENT – *The slothful man boasted not that which he took in hunting: but the substance of a diligent man is precious. Proverbs 12:27*
- WISE – *We are fools for Christ's sake, but ye are wise in Christ; we are weak, but ye are strong; ye are honourable but we are despised. I Corinthians 4:10*
- OVERCOMER – *For whatsoever is born of God overcometh the world: and this is the victory that overcometh the world, even our faith. I John 5:4*
- MEEK – *But let it be the hidden man of the heart, in that which is not corruptible, even the ornament of a meek and quiet spirit, which is in the sight of God of great*

price. I Peter 3:4

- ANOINTED – *Now he which established us with you in Christ and hath anointed us, is God. II Corinthians 1:21*
- NEW – *Therefore if any man be in Christ, he is a new creature. Old things are passed away behold all things are become new. II Corinthians 5:17*

These are some of the qualities of a fully committed Demolition Woman.

A Message to a Demolition Woman

Whether single or married, you have endured your trials. In the midst of your greatest battles and warfare, something wonderful happened. The Lord our God developed you as a mighty woman of God. You are full of grace and power. You are a beautiful woman of God. You are the workmanship of God. You were designed to bring and show forth the beauty of God. However, you were also designed to be warriors of God.

God is calling you to a higher level in this century. Go back and read the Word of God again. God is speaking wonderful things about women and giving examples throughout out the Bible of provisions He made for women.

Therefore, you do not have to believe the lie that you are not called or chosen. You were called and chosen. You were created for greatness. God put Adam to sleep and made woman (Eve) Genesis 2:21-23. Adam had nothing to do with her makeup. You were designed by God. You were made out of substance.

A DEMOLITION WOMAN MUST DESTROY low self-esteem in her life and walk in her God-given rights.

It is time for you to feel good about yourself and your accomplishments. As you submit to God, the enemy in your life must go. DEMOLITION WOMAN, you are called to rise up in this hour. Be what God has called you to be. Do not allow anyone to hinder the move of God in your life. If you have been called to pastor and you know it, so be it. Start moving towards your goal. If God has called you to teach and you know it, prepare yourself and do it with all your might.

If God has called you to establish a soup kitchen, so be it. If God has called you to the apostleship ministry, so be it. Establish and set in order the house of God. If God has called you a prophetess, so be it. Speak prophetically to the nation. Not only has God called you a D-E-MO-L-I-T-I-O-N W-O-M-AN, He has delegated authority to you. Now it is up to you to walk in it. You are anointed, chosen, called, qualified and dangerous to the enemy's plan.

DEMOLITION WOMAN, you are commissioned for this hour, seize the hour.